A QUARTER-CENTURY
of
SOCIOLOGY
at the
UNIVERSITY
OF TORONTO
1963-1988

A Commemorative Volume with Essays by
S.D. Clark and Oswald Hall

Edited by R. Helmes-Hayes

Canadian Scholars' Press   Toronto   1988

First published in 1988 by

Canadian Scholars' Press Inc.
211 Grenadier Road
Toronto, Canada
M6R 1R9

Canadian Cataloguing in Publication Data

Main entry under title:
A Quarter-century of Sociology at the University of Toronto 1963-1988

Bibliography: p.
ISBN 0-921627-07-6

1. University of Toronto. Dep't. of Sociology — History. 2. Sociology — Study and teaching (Higher) — Ontario — Toronto. I. Helmes-Hayes, Richard C. (Richard Charles), 1951- .

HM47.C22T68 1988   301'.07'11713541   C88-095217-2

TABLE OF CONTENTS

EDITOR'S INTRODUCTION

As its title may be a trifle deceiving, it should be noted at the outset that this little book does not provide a comprehensive, critical history of the University of Toronto Department of Sociology since 1963. That is not its purpose. Instead, it has been put together as a memento intended to celebrate the Department's twenty-fifth anniversary.

Those with even a passing familiarity with the history of the Department will know that, as in all departments of sociology, there have been stormy and difficult times at Toronto. The conflicts between individuals and factions over issues normally referred to as 'office' or 'departmental politics' tend in departments such as sociology to be rendered more Byzantine in their complexity and more difficult of resolution by the fact that sociology is an inherently 'political' discipline in the broader sense of that term. Thus, at Toronto as elsewhere, matters of day-to-day administration become tangled in wider political disputes to a degree that they do not in other disciplines and departments in the university. Such matters, while worthy of sociological investigation, are not addressed in this volume and so readers looking for a muck-making exposé — the inside story of what *really* happened between 1963 and 1988 — will be disappointed by the contents of the book. In a volume written on short notice and intended to be commemorative, if not mildly celebratory, a detailed, critical history of the department seemed both impossible and inappropriate.

This does not mean that the book is barren of historical or sociological interest. It contains much that historians of sociology will find useful; year-by-year lists of teaching staff and Ph.D dissertations (by year) as well as original essays about the department written by two of its distinguished, long-time members, S.D. Clark and Oswald Hall. Professor Simpson and I chose Professors Clark and Hall to contribute to the volume on the grounds that they alone among a number of eminent senior members of the Department are Professors Emeriti of the University, Fellows of the Royal Society of Canada, and Honorary Presidents of the Canadian Sociology and Anthropology Association. Students of the history of sociology

iii

and those with a more casual interest in the history of the department will alike find their essays to be absorbing reading. Professor Clark's essay, "How the Department of Sociology Came Into Being," recounts the early (pre-1963) development of sociology at the University of Toronto from the point of view of one who was an 'insider' to the process. Professor Hall's contribution, "Some Recollections of Sociology in Two Universities: McGill and the University of Toronto," draws on his experience in the two departments to offer us — again from an insider's vantage point — a systematic comparison of selected aspects of the development of sociology at McGill and the University of Toronto. Without reading too much into either of their essays, it is fair to say, I think, that they hint at some of the contentious issues that a careful scholarly analysis of the Department's history would involve. Toronto has long been a major center of academic sociology in Canada and so a full-scale history of the Department, while difficult, would certainly be an interesting and useful undertaking.

By way of closing, I would like to offer some points of information about the volume and to thank some of the people who were involved in its preparation.

I gathered the information in Chapters 3 and 4 and Appendices A and B. I was assisted in various ways by different people in the preparation of this material and I have acknowledged their help where appropriate. Any errors or ommissions are my responsibility.

For their assistance during the course of the carrying out of this project I would like to offer special thanks to Professors John Simpson, S.D. Clark and Oswald Hall. I am indebted to Professor Simpson on two counts. First, he was a helpful and encouraging 'ghost editor'. Second, by engaging me to oversee the production of this little book, he offered me the chance to interact with two of the makers of Canadian sociology. This allowed me the rare opportunity to experience a little of the history of the discipline as close to 'first-hand' as is possible without actually having been there. For their part, Professors Hall and Clark made it a valuable learning experience. They were gracious and generous in their responses to my often naive queries about the history of Canadian sociology and I would like to thank them for their patience and assistance.

As a final note, I want to thank Drs. Richard Schmidt and Gabrielle MacDonald of the Writing Lab at New College,

University of Toronto and Michael Parker of the Classics Department of Memorial University for 'technical' editorial assistance.

R. Helmes-Hayes
August 1988

CHAIRMAN'S INTRODUCTION

This small volume commemorates the twenty-fifth anniversary of the establishment of the Department of Sociology in the University of Toronto. It is not, as the editor points out, a history of the Department of sociology at Toronto. It does make available some facts and interpretations that should cause the work of writing a history of the Department to be easier than would otherwise have been the case. Thus, this volume points to the future as much as it memorializes the past.

The volume had its origin in a meeting of Professors Dennis Magill and Lorna Marsden and myself in the fall of 1987 where the general contents were outlined. Given his key interest in the history of sociology in Canada and his scholarly credentials, it was agreed that Dr. Rick Helmes-Hayes should be invited to serve as editor. Fortunately, he accepted our offer. His superb research and editorial skills have brought our ideas to fruition. By way of friendly comment on Dr. Helmes-Hayes' introduction to this volume I would note that in my experience not all departments of sociology are politically feisty nor is sociology any more inherently political in the broad sense of that term than many other university disciplines.

Special thanks are due Professors Emeriti S.D. Clark and Oswald Hall for agreeing to write the essays appearing herein. They are rich sources of insight into the milieux which have influenced the department and into the dynamics of its collective life.

For those readers who are not members of the professional company of sociologists this volume provides some insight in to the nature of the sociological task and its implementation at Toronto.

For sociologists in Canada and elsewhere this volume provides some data that may prove useful for assessing the contribution of sociology at Toronto to the discipline so far.

John H. Simpson
September 1988

CHAPTER 1

HOW THE DEPARTMENT OF SOCIOLOGY CAME INTO BEING

S.D. CLARK

By stretching a point it could be said that sociology had its beginning, at the University of Toronto at least, in 1915. It was in that year that R.M. MacIver joined the faculty of the university. As a lecturer in political philosophy at the University of Aberdeen before coming to Toronto, as he relates in his autobiography, *As a Tale that is Told*, MacIver had developed a strong interest in sociology and his continued interest in the area while at Toronto was evident in the extended revision of his sociological study, *The Community*. It was only after moving to Columbia University in 1927, however, that he gained recognition as a sociologist. At the University of Toronto all his teaching was in the area of political science and he appears to have had no influence upon the later development of sociology at this university.

To E.J. Urwick belongs the credit for the establishment of a teaching programme in sociology at the University of Toronto. After retiring from the London School of Economics and Political Science as a professor of social philosophy, Urwick had come to Canada with the intention of settling in Vancouver (he was a man of private means). However, a bitter struggle between two senior professors for the headship of what was then known as the Department of Political Science on MacIver's leaving led Sir Robert Falconer, the president of the university, to persuade Urwick to assume the post. Soon after, he was also appointed Acting Director of the School of Social Work, then known as the Department of Social Science, a position he was to hold (as a result of the prolonged illness of the director) until his retirement from the university .

It was primarily to provide a background of training for students entering social work (then a one-year diploma programme after the B.A.) which led to Urwick's interest in 1933 in establishing an honours programme in sociology. To anyone not familiar with the thinking in the university at the time it might appear strange that an honours course in sociology was

1

set up before there was a single person in the school to teach the discipline. But among the founders of the course, including Urwick (and the new president of the university, Canon Cody), sociology was not thought of as an independent area of study; rather, it was conceived of as a distinctive grouping of a number of different areas: political science, philosophy, history, psychology, anthropology, and zoology. A committee was established to administer the programme made up of faculty members drawn from these different areas of the university, with Urwick as chairman.

No sociology was offered in the first year of the programme. Students with the intention of honouring in sociology took courses in what was known as social and philosophical studies. As the first cohort of students moved into the second year, however, it was necessary to secure someone to teach a course in introductory sociology. C.W.M. Hart, a lecturer in anthropology, with a strong interest in sociology, was given this task.

If Urwick, with his strong background in social philosophy, had doubts about the claims of sociology as a science, those doubts were not shared by Hart. Brought close to the great master of sociology, Emile Durkheim, through Radcliffe-Brown, Hart taught a rigourously positivistic and functionally oriented sociology to his students in Toronto. It was not the kind of sociology which found favour in many quarters of the university. In Victoria College, because of the moral relativism in Hart's teachings, students were put under heavy pressure by the registrar to avoid entering the sociology honours programme. Hart, however, very much the charismatic teacher, quickly gathered a following among those students who came in contact with him and the effect of his teaching was to establish the discipline of sociology as a recognized area of study within the university. Though it was Urwick who brought into being the honours programme, to Hart should go the credit as the founder of sociology as a discipline at the University of Toronto.

In 1937 the first body of students graduated in honours sociology. By then the staff could be considered as consisting of three persons: C.W.M. Hart, E.J. Urwick and David Ketchum. Hart now taught a fourth year as well as second year course in sociology and, while still holding an appointment as Lecturer in Anthropology, had been named as Supervisor of Studies in

2

Sociology. Urwick, rather curiously described as Professor of Economics, taught a fourth year course on the history of social welfare. Ketchum, an Assistant Professor of Psychology with a Ph.D. in social psychology and sociology from the University of Chicago, offered a fourth year course on human ecology. In addition, engaged in the final year of study for my Ph.D., I was called upon to teach a third year course on the history of sociological theory (the only course in sociology yet offered in the third year). Together with these five courses, students were required to take, after social and philosophical studies, courses in economics, economic history, psychology, history, philosophy, anthropology and zoology. There were no options. In offering a broad range of training, it was a truly excellent honours programme.

Until 1938 no one teaching courses in sociology except J.G. Franz, an instructor for the year 1937-38, held a teaching appointment in sociology as such. Hart was in anthropology, Ketchum in psychology and Urwick in political economy. To begin in 1938, however, it was decided by the committee in charge of the honours programme to appoint a full-time lecturer in sociology. The result of the deliberations that ensued determined to an extent the direction sociology was to take in its development in the university. E.A. Bott, head of the Department of Psychology, proposed the appointment of one of his students who was taking his Ph.D. in sociology at the University of Chicago. My appointment, with a year of teaching at the University of Manitoba coming to an end, was proposed by H.A. Innis, head of the Department of Political Economy. Had Bott succeeded, sociology at the University of Toronto, like that at McGill at the time, almost certainly would have come under the influence of what at the time was known as the "Chicago school" of sociology. But Urwick, the chairman of the committee in charge of the honours programme, disliked Chicago sociology. As a consequence, acting on Innis' advice, he recommended to the President my appointment as a lecturer in sociology.

The future of sociology in the university, however, was not thereby wholly resolved. As a university lecturer I had to be attached for administrative purposes to a department (only departments had budgets). Since Hart's appointment was in anthropology, it was decided to attach me to the same department. All that this meant, however, was that my salary became part of anthropology's budget. It was to Urwick rather than to the head of the anthropology department, T.F. McIlwraith, that I was actually responsible. To make still more ambiguous my position, I was assigned an office in the old McMaster Building on Bloor Street occupied by the Department of Political Economy, a goodly distance from anthropology's quarters in the Royal Ontario Museum which could be reached only by means of the main door on Queen's Park Crescent.

Already as well, however, Hart's position was becoming increasingly ambiguous. All the teaching in sociology was carried on in the McMaster Building and it was in this building that Hart came to have his main office. To neither of us, as a result, did the relationship with anthropology appear to make sense. It was to Innis, head of the department of political economy, that we tended to turn for academic advice. Accordingly, sometime late in the year 1939, we approached him with the proposal that sociology should be incorporated in his department. The proposal, when put before the honours course committee, met a not wholly favourable response. Some of the members of the committee, with unkindly feelings toward what was considered "the empire of political economy," were of the view that sociology should become a separate department. In the end it was decided that for a period of two years the Department of Political Economy be put in charge of sociology. After two years the committee would meet again when consideration would be given to the establishment of a separate department.

What the members of the committee failed to take into consideration was that in approving the transfer of sociology (including the responsibility for the supervision of the honours programme) to political economy, the committee as such ceased to exist. The only person who could have re-convened it was Urwick, its chairman, and before the two years were up he was no longer with the university. An attempt on the part of other members of the committee to raise the question of the place of sociology in the university would have been considered an intrusion into the affairs of the Department of Political Economy, and Innis was not the kind of person to brook such an intrusion. It was, thus, more than twenty years before any further serious consideration was given to the creation of a department of sociology.

4

Sociology, on its transfer to political economy, did not thereby lose its stature as a distinctive discipline. Now began to emerge what could be considered as a sociology staff. Within two years time there was no one teaching a course in sociology who did not hold an appointment in the subject. Hart became an assistant professor of sociology rather than of anthropology. Ketchum in 1941 ceased to teach the fourth year course on human ecology which he had been offering, though he continued to teach in the Department of Psychology a third year course on social psychology which honour students in sociology were required to take. Urwick retired from the university, now finally settling in Vancouver. I was joined in 1940 by E.C. Devereux, a student of Talcott Parsons in Harvard, who was appointed an instructor in sociology (appointment as an instructor was simply a means of avoiding the payment of the minimum salary for a lecturer, $1800).

Our location for the first four years on the northeast corner of the second floor of the McMaster building gave the staff in sociology a sense of being an autonomous group. We had our own honours programme which remained distinct from that of economics and political science. Later we had as well our general course programme. A steadily growing programme of graduate studies leading to the M.A. and ultimately to the Ph.D. was organized and directed by the staff. Only in one important regard was the autonomy of sociology limited. It did not have its own budget and what funds were available for new appointments were determined by the head of the department (as were salary increases). While sociology faced the constraints of the departmental budget, the staff in sociology was given an almost completely free hand in recommending new appointments.

The nineteen-forties and -fifties were not years of rapid university growth and the slow expansion of the staff in sociology was a reflection of this fact. After two years at Toronto, with the United States now in the war, Devereux in 1942 was called up by the American navy, his place taken by Aileen Ross, who remained on the staff for the next three years before returning to her home town, Montreal, and McGill University. The hiring of Eva Younge in 1943-44 and D.G. Marshall in 1944-45 as sessional appointments allowed Hart and I to secure the teaching of sociology's complement of honours courses. The building up of what might be described as the regular staff

5

began in 1945 with the appointment of J.R. Burnet as an instructor who, after spending the year 1948-49 at the University of New Brunswick, returned to Toronto as a lecturer. Her appointment was followed by that of P.J. Giffen in 1948 and L. Zakuta in 1952. S.M. Lipset spent the first two years of his teaching career at Toronto, 1946-48, and Eli Chinoy the first four years, 1947-51. For the three years, 1951-54, Norman Ryder was a member of the staff, and for the two years 1951-53 J.C. Riemersma from Holland who, with training in both chemistry and the social sciences, went on from Toronto to Berkeley to teach economic history and then returned to his native land to take up his research interest in the field of chemistry. Also holding appointments in sociology in 1950-54, but without salary, were J.R. Seeley and R.A. Sim who, holding a mental health research grant from the federal government, were on the staff of the Department of Psychiatry while carrying out the *Crestwood Heights* study. Hart left in 1948 to accept an appointment at the University of Wisconsin, and in 1956 Oswald Hall joined the staff to be followed by N. Keyfitz in 1959, H.K. Nishio in 1961 and R.C. Beals, R.A. Lucas and D.E. Willmott in 1962. In addition to such distinguished visitors as Robert E. Park, Talcott Parsons, R.K. Merton, Helen McGill Hughes, and C.A. Dawson, Theodor Geiger was a visiting professor in 1951-52, Sir A. Carr-Saunders in 1960-61 and Morris Ginsberg in the spring term of 1948. In 1962-63 the staff consisted of eight full-time members. Keyfitz was on leave that year, to accept an appointment at the University of Chicago the next year, while Nishio, to comply with U.S. immigration regulations, did not take up a regular appointment at Toronto until 1964. Though his name appeared on the staff list as a special lecturer, R.J. Coughlin was in fact a member of the faculty of newly established York University which, for the year 1962-63, under the conditions of its founding, was affiliated with the University of Toronto. Coughlin did, however, take part in a monthly staff seminar held on an informal basis in the homes of different members of the faculty.

With Vincent Bladen, C.A. Ashley and W.T. Easterbrook coming after Innis, the staff in sociology was fortunate in its chairmen (now no longer known as heads). There were distinct advantages in being a part of political economy. While sociology's image may have suffered in some quarters outside

Toronto as a result of its seeming lack of independence as an administrative unit, the tie with political economy very much enhanced its image within the university. The department was one which was highly regarded in the university administration. The gain to sociology was particularly evident in the development of its graduate programme. In contrast to proposals from some departments, proposals going forward from sociology to the School of Graduate Studies generally gained ready acceptance. There were other advantages as well in being a part of political economy, not the least of which was avoiding the administrative chores involved in the management of a department.

If the tie with political economy served to strengthen the position of sociology in the University of Toronto, in many ways it served as well to strengthen its position in the Canadian academic community at large. While Toronto sociology may well have been looked at askance in some sociological quarters, its standing as a discipline was greatly enhanced from its association with such highly regarded scholars as Harold Innis. The first appointments in sociology in Saskatchewan, New Brunswick and Victoria College in British Columbia were of persons who had done there graduate work in Toronto. As well, close ties were established with McMaster University and the University of Manitoba.

One of the major activities undertaken by the staff in sociology was the establishment, with a grant from the Rockefeller foundation, of a two-day seminar which met once a year over a three-year period, beginning in 1955, devoted to a discussion of a major issue in sociology. Sociologists were invited, with their expenses paid, from the different universities in Ontario and Quebec. Also attending were some people from federal government departments. The first seminar was built around the subject of population, with Kingsley Davis as a special guest. There followed a seminar on elites with C. Wright Mills in attendance and one on small-group sociology with George Homans. It was at the last meeting of the seminar that steps were taken to organize the sociology chapter of the Canadian Political Science Association, a development which led ultimately to the establishment, in 1965, of the Canadian Sociology and Anthropology Association.

Throughout the years leading up to the establishment of the department in 1963 members of the staff were engaged in a

7

number of research studies. It was while at Toronto that Lipset carried to completion his study on agrarian socialism and Chinoy his study of automobile workers. Burnet, following up on her study of an Alberta rural community, turned to a concern with the relationship of systems of moral values to the changing structure of the Canadian society, while Giffen turned from a study of the legal profession to an interest in studying deviant forms of behaviour. Zakuta moved from a study of the C.C.F. in Ontario to an examination of interpersonal relations in society. Hall, after coming to Toronto, followed up on his study of the medical profession to the general area of the sociology of work while Keyfitz carried forward his work on South East Asia. My own interest in the development of the Canadian society led to studies of sectarian religious movements and movements of political protest in Canada over time, and to a study of the suburban society.

At various times before 1962, in no very serious way, the question was mooted whether sociology should become a separate department. The respective chairmen of political economy — Innis, Bladen, Ashley and Easterbrook — were not in favour of separation, and no move was made by members of the sociology staff which would have led to such a development. The close personal ties which over the years had become established between the members of the sociology staff and other members of the staff in the political economy department, more particularly on the part of the younger members of the department situated on the fourth floor of the old McMaster Building, had built up very much a sense of community. On academic grounds, the view was strongly held by the department of the value of the close association between economics, political science, commerce and finance, and sociology.

In the course of the year 1962-63, however, a marked change occurred in the position of sociology in the Department of Political Economy. The department had in 1960 taken up quarters in Sidney Smith Hall and, with the expansion now beginning to occur in the university, it grew to over one hundred and fifty staff members. It took one of the largest rooms in Sidney Smith Hall to accommodate a faculty meeting. Members of the sociology staff, scattered as they were on the third floor among economists, political scientists and commerce and finance people, began to lose a sense of belonging to a community.

It was, however, a development outside political economy which precipitated the move which led to the establishment of a separate department of sociology. By 1963 Sidney Smith Hall had become so crowded that it could no longer accommodate all the departments that had been housed there in 1960. Volunteers were called for to move to the Borden Building which had just been taken over by the university. Given some interest on the part of the members of the sociology staff in making such a move, Oswald Hall and I paid a visit to the building. The only way we could gain entry was by crawling through an unlocked basement window. Our not unfavourable report led to the decision to inform Dean Bladen that we were prepared to make the move. Sidney Smith Hall, with its windowless inside offices and at the time without air conditioning, held little attraction for its occupants. Eventually the Departments of Anthropology and Islamic Studies were asked by the Dean to move with us. We were assigned accommodation on the second and third floors of the building, with the university police occupying the first floor.

In moving to the Borden Building the expectation was that we would remain a part of the Department of Political Economy. Once the planning of the office accommodation in the building was underway, however, the awkwardness of the situation became apparent. The President of the university, Claude Bissell, had made it known that he thought sociology should become a separate department and a chance discussion between Hall and me led to the discovery that we both favoured such a move. There followed a meeting of all the members of the staff in the main lounge of the faculty club and it was decided to seek the establishment of a separate department. Accordingly, Hall and I met with Easterbrook, the chairman of the Department of Political Economy, and Bladen, the Dean of the Faculty of Arts and Sciences, to convey the views of the sociology staff. Easterbrook was very much against sociology moving out of political economy, holding the view that economic history required its presence in the department to offset the growing dominance of theoretical economics. Bladen, however, in his usual decisive manner, acted on the request of the sociology staff and recommended to the President the establishment in the university of a department of sociology.

The department came into being July 1, 1963, with myself as Chairman and Mrs. Sorenson as secretary. We took up our office quarters, together with anthropology, on the second floor of the Borden Building, with Islamic Studies located on the third. All that remained was the establishment of the department's budget. The university budget for the year 1963-64 had already been passed by the board of governors. It was necessary, therefore, for the dean to transfer to sociology some of political economy's funds. For 1964-65 sociology secured its own budget. By then the staff had grown to fifteen people; this growth was to continue unabated for the next ten years.

CHAPTER 2

SOME RECOLLECTIONS OF SOCIOLOGY IN TWO UNIVERSITIES: MCGILL AND THE UNIVERSITY OF TORONTO

OSWALD HALL

In the preceding chapter S.D. Clark has documented the steps through which sociology at the University of Toronto became an official department. By an interesting coincidence Professor Marlene Shore, in her recent volume, *The Science of Social Redemption*, has traced the early decades of the Department of Sociology at McGill, in particular the formative period, 1920-1940. Since these two departments soon became the leaders of sociology in Canada it is of interest to compare and contrast how the subject gained a place in each university. In other words, how did the larger enterprise, sociology as a realm of research and a field of teaching, become established as an enduring part of these universities?

In attempting such a comparison I have depended on a set of personal recollections. These range in age from half a century to a quarter of a century, and are often the worse for wear. As noted above the efforts of Clark and Shore are based on archival records, and stand at the other pole as far as documentation is concerned. The best I can claim is an effort to use a sociological perspective to maintain a depersonalized view of the emergence of these two departments.

During their formative years these two departments of sociology had minimal contacts with each other. Geographical distance and the demands on time and energy contributed to an 'arm's-length' relationship between them. On the other hand, this was not true of the two universities. On this larger scene there was vigorous rivalry between the two institutions. This was especially marked between their respective schools of social work, each of which played a consequential role in the emergence of sociology and its efforts to establish a distinctive identity.

Forty years elapsed between the establishment of a department at McGill and one at Toronto. That at McGill emerged during the post-war depression of the Twenties, and developed its distinctive character during the Great Depression of the Thirties. That at Toronto began to take form during the Great Depression, but achieved formal status only later, during a period of prosperity and optimism on the Ontario scene.

The issues addressed in this essay can be summarized as follows. In what ways can its distinctive urban environment impinge on an emerging department of sociology? What are the peculiar circumstances faced by the discipline as it finds acceptance in the academic community? How does a consensus arise as to what will be taught, and be the subject of research, in the new discipline? In what ways can the teaching enterprise be structured to transmit the discipline to future generations? What administrative arrangements in the university facilitate the growth of a new discipline? And what are the elements of morale and *esprit de corps* which favour the success of the sociological enterprise?

The Urban Settings

The place of sociology at McGill tended to mirror the place of McGill in Montreal. McGill is a private university, an orphan child as far as the city of Montreal and the province of Quebec are concerned. The department, like the university, was perpetually short of resources, both physical and budgetary. The struggle for survival was genuine.

On the other hand Montreal was a laboratory tailor-made for sociological research; especially for those who enjoy studying society 'on the hoof'. It was a city with a cosmopolitan flavour and a readily grasped structure. Mountains and rivers hemmed it in, thus denying it the luxury of the urban sprawl so common on this continent. Its geography and history had combined to make it a grand hub of water and rail transportation. History had endowed it with the great head offices of finance, commerce and industry which in turn dominated the affairs of half a continent.

Like many other North American cities it was a product of migration. The new population groups had generated an elaborate social structure. On its map the two dominant groups, Francophones and Anglophones, were sharply divided

12

by an unmarked line. Within these two divisions there had emerged enclaves of minority groups. The shoulders of the mountain (Mount Royal) tended to parallel the social classes of the city. Where residential areas collided with commercial areas one could readily locate the human casualties of city life, the poor, the unemployed, the disorganized, and those on the wrong side of the law. Economic classes and social classes all had a recognizable location in the structure of the city.

The city of Montreal presented intriguing research queries for a sociologist. How and where do migrant newcomers find a place to settle? How do they attach themselves to work opportunities? How do they prepare their children for such challenges? How do racial, ethnic, and religious minorities maintain (or surrender) their cultural bonds? How do they sort and sift themselves with respect to the occupational and industrial structure of the city? Montreal was both an intriguing social laboratory and an exciting cosmopolitan city in which to live.

Toronto, as the locale for an emerging department of sociology, presented a vastly different visage. It could hardly claim cosmopolitan status. Rather, it retained much of the character of a provincial town. On the other hand, it gave promise of enormous sprawl to the east, the north, and the west. Moreover, it was marked by strong population growth, particularly of European migrants, in the wake of the Second World War. But with the exception of a Chinatown any sharply defined areas of ethnic concentration scarcely existed. Where they could be detected they tended to have rapidly shifting borders. Toronto lacked the tiny enclaves of ethnic and religious groupings which Montreal exhibited (and which invited sociological attention).

On closer observation it was evident that while Toronto had not become a cosmopolitan city it was on its way to becoming a metropolitan centre. Unlike Montreal it had developed as the hub of a constellation of smaller cities. Whereas Montreal was essentially self-contained for Toronto much of the relevant commerce and industry was dispersed in a system of encircling communities. General Motors to the east and Ford to the west had generated distinctive satellite cities. Hence Toronto was essentially the centre of an increasingly large constellation of vigorous and wealthy communities. Moreover the University of Toronto was also on the way to becoming the centre of an increasingly large constellation of universities and colleges.

While McGill, as a private institution, was fundamentally a product of a narrowly based upper class in Montreal, and had generated hostile relations with the Government of Quebec, the University of Toronto was a provincially supported institution. Moreover, the Government of Ontario was increasingly disposed to support education in general and this support flowed toward universities. While McGill routinely faced a bleak future with regard to financial support the University of Toronto suffered little in the way of such constraints. It could afford a department of sociology.

Without stressing the point unduly, it can be confidently asserted that the geographical setting helped define sociology in the two universities. At McGill the classical problems of urban sociology lay bare to view on the body of the city, within reach of a streetcar ride. At Toronto they were scattered and concealed in a metropolitan community, its satellite cities, and its extended hinterland.

The Emergence of Sociology

On both campuses one can trace early tentative steps to establish sociology, as well as the official efforts to find it a place in the university. At Toronto two developments are noteworthy — the creation of an honours course in sociology in the Thirties, and the establishment of an autonomous department three decades later. At McGill these two developments were telescoped.

It is usual to equate the beginning of sociology at McGill with the name of one man, Carl Dawson. He came to McGill at a point when the School of Social Work was struggling over the relative importance of research and social action. Others outside the school were also involved in the struggle, persons in administration, and economists such as Stephen Leacock. (As a matter of record, his *Sunshine Sketches of a Little Town* was first-class small town sociology).

Marlene Shore was much impressed by Dawson's crusading zeal for sociology and his single-minded efforts to create a department dedicated to teaching and research. She attributed his congenial conversion to sociology as a product of his Baptist background, since she sees in that religion a ready affinity with scientific orientations. A more convincing argument can be made that Dawson was deeply influenced by sheer mobility — both his own and others'. His early background was that of the most stable social system in Canada — Prince Edward Island. Family systems and farm family systems had there generated a secure environment. The years that Dawson spent later in the Western prairies, as a school teacher, were a vivid contrast. Incidentally, he returned there a decade later to study systematically the family systems and settlement processes that had earlier attracted his attention. The impact of the First World War, and his experiences with returning soldiers, contrasted vividly with the security of his own early years. Later, when he went to the University of Chicago, he encountered a tumultuous, impersonal city. Previous observers had noted that "city air makes man free." This it did for Dawson. There he developed an intensely interested, but highly detached, concern with urban life, freed of attachment to any enterprise except sociology. Other teachers at McGill could become embroiled in social movements, reform movements, and political movements, but he created for himself a core of scholarly detachment.

Although he was saddled initially at McGill with the administration of the School of Social Work he quickly shed those responsibilities in order to concentrate on sociology. His strategy was two-fold; to emphasize the teaching of a sociology with a Canadian flavour, and to pursue research into what he considered consequential problems on the Canadian scene. In his eyes the two enterprises were interlinked. Because there were few teaching materials at hand, he co-authored an introductory textbook, one which had a durable academic life. Thereafter, he engaged in research, particularly with respect to the dynamics of Canadian population growth and movements and the settlement of new parts of Canada. On a large canvas he promoted research through the activities of the Social Science Research Council and the cooperation of philanthropic foundations. As time went on very useful teaching materials emerged, such as E.C. Hughes' *French Canada in Transition* and Horace Miner's *St. Denis*. For his own part he generated a series of general articles as well as four volumes on Western Canada.

In the sociology courses which he generated at McGill the research interest blended with the teaching interest. The students were encouraged and challenged to explore the society around them, and to view it through a sociological lens. Initially there were two foci of this enterprise. Students were stimulated to explore, in a detailed way, the families of which they were a part, and also to explore the distinctive neighbourhoods in which they participated. For most of these students sociology became a much more lively enterprise than the book learning which they encountered in most other departments.

The interest in sociology was most lively and intense among students who registered in the honours program. In those courses student interest pyramided upon student interest, and as a result there was a steady growth in graduate courses leading to the M.A. degree. The research interest helped to create the degree, which in turn placed major emphasis on the research thesis. The graduate students became field sociologists who created substantial research documents while at the same time arming themselves for significant careers as sociologists. In the latter years of his life at McGill Dawson could savour the success of his research-teaching career. The late Forties saw an impressive cohort of graduate students, a large number of whom later chaired departments of sociology.

The emergence of sociology at the University of Toronto has been chronicled by Professor Clark, but it may be useful to pursue comparisons with McGill. If at McGill the genesis of the department partook of the nature of an immaculate conception, at Toronto the metaphor would be that of a protracted Caesarean section, perhaps the longest on record.

At McGill the sociology program emerged as an effort to achieve academic distance from social work; at Toronto it was designed as an important supplement of social work teaching. Slowly and gradually this bond dissolved both as an administrative arrangement and as a focus of teaching. Initially those teaching sociology were drawn from a variety of fields, and worked under the umbrella of the Department of Anthropology. Eventually the teaching staff comprised solely sociologists, but by this time they worked under the Department of Political Economy.

At McGill sociology was represented by someone who was by training and conviction undoubtedly a sociologist. Dawson had studied at an impressive department of sociology (the University of Chicago) and was ranked as one of its top graduates. He had a sturdy sense of being an authentic representative of his discipline, and he determined, as the department grew, to add only recognized sociologists of comparable stature. By contrast, the Toronto venture began by collecting a team of teachers. These were of diverse backgrounds, including an anthropologist, an economist, and a psychologist, plus Professor Clark who had studied undergraduate history, proceeded to the London School of Economics and moved to McGill to study sociology for two years. After seven years the economist and psychologist were dispensed with. The anthropologist continued for another seven years, by which time the program was an unambiguously sociological enterprise. Unlike Dawson at McGill there had been no initiating figure to impose a homogeneous character on the program. To a large degree the sociologists took guidance from the larger department, one which encouraged a high degree of freedom for teachers to devise their own courses.

The Sociology Curricula

The structure of a department is little more than a framework around which the program coalesces. The formation of a new discipline in the university rests on the recognition of a new participant in the division of labour in the field of knowledge. It also rests on a degree of consensus among the teachers in that field as to what the core of the new discipline comprises.

As noted above, the program at Toronto was by its nature eclectic. The four initiating teachers brought diverse backgrounds to the common task. Since the objective at the beginning was to supplement the training of social workers, a broadly based set of courses was readily justified. The range of interests of the instructors was impressive. One member brought an orientation from social philosophy, with a European flavour. Another had trained in anthropology, with a focus on preliterate peoples. The third was a professional psychologist who had developed an interest in human ecology during his studies at the University of Chicago. The fourth brought a broad acquaintance with Canadian society, and with his background in history, political science and sociology, could be properly described as an historically oriented social scientist.

17

While such an array of courses could well serve the needs of students in social work, they were untidy bedfellows as far as an authentic department of sociology was concerned. As time went on only one of these orientations survived, that of historically oriented sociology. As the others disappeared from the program, formally trained sociologists with an acquaintance with the Canadian scene took their place. Thereafter the students in sociology had the opportunity to explore such fields as population, minority groups, political movements, and legal and health care systems. As mentioned earlier these developments took place within a department of political economy, one which encouraged the intermingling of a variety of disciplines, and which also provided a maximum of autonomy for teachers to create their own distinctive courses. Hence there was little pressure to generate a "Toronto school" of sociology.

The contrast with McGill has been foreshadowed in the preceding section. At McGill sociology was no adjunct of social work, but rather a repudiation of any such ties.It also turned resolutely away from the "Social Problems" view of sociology as a study of crime, delinquency, suicide, prostitution, poverty, and such matters. Dawson viewed sociology as a thoroughly autonomous field of study with its own foci of attention and the corresponding obligation to carry out research therein.

Very early in his work at McGill he co-authored an introductory textbook which indicated the directions in which the department would evolve. His central course work would concentrate on the community, particularly the urban community. To this would be added courses on population and migration of peoples. Whereas these courses would reflect an ecological approach they would be supplemented with courses dealing with culture. Eventually teachers of cultural anthropology would be added to the department. (In Toronto these were separated in distinctive departments.) At McGill there were further courses to be added dealing with the family (Dawson originally taught this course) and courses on the socialization of the child in the family. Dawson also pursued this field in the direction of adult socialization, in his course on social attitudes. While all of these courses can be viewed as an integrated view of a society, Dawson also realized that there are dramatic and even revolutionary changes occurring, which may shatter the structure of a social system. Hence courses were added in the general field of social movements as a counterpart to those just described.

Note was made earlier of the teaching orientation of courses in sociology at McGill — the dual emphasis on library work and field study. Students were exposed to the classical literature, insofar as the library resources permitted, but were vigorously encouraged to supplement this approach by an attempt to gather raw data as an integral part of the sociological enterprise. Dawson held the notion that "to be a sociologist is to know something about something". In his eyes well-grounded knowledge emerged from field research. This emphasis tended to put sociology in a special place on the campus, since most other departments relied almost entirely on library resources. This dual orientation in sociology had a salutary effect on the work for the M.A. degree. For that program all students were required to complete a dissertation based on empirical data. In other departments and in other universities students could obtain this degree by course credits solely. The McGill policy regarding the M.A. program contributed greatly to the reputation for research in general which the department enjoyed.

The Teaching Enterprise

The teaching of sociology at McGill had something of a collective character, both in the planning of courses and in the teaching and assessing of students. This could be noted on three levels. The large courses, in which there were various sections, were organized on a unified framework of common readings. All students would end up with a roughly comparable background in sociology, as a prelude to succeeding courses. While each teacher generated his or her own teaching style, there was a sturdy common core. Students and teachers had a common understanding of what each course entailed.

In these courses use was made of graduate student teaching assistants. These met students to discuss both reading materials and the term projects noted earlier. They also participated in the grading of reports and examinations. This arrangement required close collaboration among the assistants as well as with the relevant faculty members.

Further collective energy went into the planning of the curriculum as a whole, and the integration of its parts. Where faculty enjoyed a common background in their own graduate

19

work this was easily managed. Where their backgrounds differed, as occurred when social anthropologists and sociologists devised a common course, the collaboration was more arduous. The result, it was hoped, was a more unified course rather than one in which the integration of materials was left up to the student.

The manner of teaching the courses determined in large part the manner of assessing students. The assessments occurred at various stages in a course and involved, in large courses, several staff. Term projects formed an integral part of the overall assessment of the student. It was difficult for a student to get lost, or be anonymous, in such circumstances. The grading system stood at the opposite extreme from the true-false and multiple-choice examinations which were arising in other departments in the university.

In sociology at Toronto there seemed less emphasis on joint planning of courses and the integration of teachers. To some degree this pattern arose in the very beginning, when scholars of diverse orientations each contributed a course. Moreover the ethos of the department of political economy, to which sociologists belonged, strongly emphasized the individual prerogatives of faculty members to create courses on their own initiative. On the other hand the actual evaluation of grades of final examinations was eventually a collective affair, with marks passing up through a series of committees. Hence idiosyncracies in grading by specific instructors would be counteracted.

One peculiar feature of the Toronto examinations was the system of anonymity under which students wrote. Hence it was officially impossible for the instructor in a course to discover the identity of the student writing the examination. As a consequence, a teacher was precluded from seeing, at the end of a course, the progress of a student along the various stages of that course. This arrangement had stemmed from peculiar historical circumstances, and like much else would disappear around the time the department was formally established.

The Context of Administration

Professor Clark has discussed the early incorporation of sociology in the Department of Anthropology at Toronto. Soon afterwards it found a home in the Department of Political

Economy which comprised economic history, economic theory and political science. This was a congenial home with a large family of cognate subjects.

It was also a prestigious place to locate. The senior members of the department enjoyed superior reputations as scholars, and thereby added an enviable environment for the new discipline. The head of the department was an internationally acclaimed social scientist, and at the same time an energetic administrator. His research scholarship was a challenge to members of the new discipline, and his administrative skills left the sociologists free of such chores. To this should be added his role as Dean of Graduate Studies. His encouragement made it easy for the sociology department to establish a graduate program at an early stage.

The larger department provided a model for the recruitment of new members of the teaching staff in sociology. While the department sought, as occasion arose, to attract luminaries from other campuses, it also found a place for its own promising graduate students. It would be incorrect to stress unduly the role of selection from within. In large part the department provided teachers for an encircling set of comparable departments in other parts of Canada. Later these scholars might return to Toronto, having proved their competence in a different environment.

The availability of contact with other members of a heterogeneous department meant that sociologists were not restricted to fellow sociologists for companionship. Small departments tend to breed intense personal relationships, but Toronto sociologists escaped this hazard.

The generous welcome to a large department of a small body of newcomers eventually had unanticipated consequences. By the time the sociologists were prepared to go their own way they had become so important to some parts of the larger department that their going was deplored.

The incorporation of sociology at McGill took an entirely different turn. No department offered to take it under its wing. The established departments were either actively hostile to the new discipline, or questioned its credentials in a negative way. Each step on the road to acceptance had to be earned either through student recognition or by contributions to research. Moreover this was in effect a one-man enterprise. There was no counterpart to the four-man team that pioneered sociology at Toronto.

If Dawson viewed his work as something of a crusade, some of his students soon came to share this enthusiasm for the place of the new discipline. When the opportunity came to participate in research on the settlement of Western Canada, Dawson was in the enviable position of having a research orientation that was much in demand, and having a first-hand acquaintance with the area to be studied. While he made no converts among the economists involved in that research, he won grudging respect from some of them.

As Dawson looked forward to the expansion of the department he insisted adamantly on adding only established sociologists. He fought to secure colleagues rather than junior assistants. In this he battled against the recruitment policy of other McGill departments, and the vigorous opposition of deans and other administrators, who, with an eye on the budget, preferred appointments at the most junior level. Dawson aimed at an egalitarian colleague framework for a department, rather than a hierarchy of levels.

The department which he created lacked the luxury of a benevolent umbrella such as that enjoyed by sociologists of the University of Toronto. Hence Dawson had to seek out kindred spirits in the university in whatever department he could find them. There was a core of them who enjoyed fishing, skiing, and vigorous conversation. This group was expanded to include pivotally important members of the Faculty of Arts, who in due course would support Dawson's goals for his department.

That department grew from very small beginnings. One result was an atmosphere that promoted the growth of very warm collegial relationships. Professor Clark has mentioned the spatial dispersal of faculty members in the early history of sociology at Toronto. At McGill the members worked in close physical proximity. Moreover spouses and other family members came to share in the life of the department, even including teaching chores. The newly recruited members joined a warm cohesive group. The candidates for new positions visited the campus as house guests rather than hotel guests. Meal-sharing and evening parties were a norm. Day-long picnics, which included graduate students, became a veritable institution. The graduate students in turn formed their own lively seminar groups to supplement, and on occasion subvert, the formal arrangements.

In conclusion, it is clear that the McGill and Toronto departments moved toward their present levels of prominence by markedly different routes. In this essay a few of the important contingencies have been noted. The surrounding locale in which the university is set grants some opportunities and excludes others. Historical developments in other parts of the university impinge on the development of a new discipline. The legacy of those who initiate the new enterprise continues to provide direction far into the future. The emerging understandings as to what constitutes the core of a discipline, and the core activities of its representatives, constrains the development of a department. The administrative arrangements within which a department is nestled impose an imprint on that development. And, finally, the inner ethos and *esprit de corps* which accompany its emergence maintain a lingering influence on its future development.

CHAPTER 3

LIST OF TEACHING STAFF BY YEAR
1963-64 to 1987-88*

1963-64
Professors
S.D. Clark (Chair)
O. Hall
R.L. James (Visiting)
Associate Professor
P.J. Giffen
Assistant Professors
J.R. Burnet
D. Reuschemeyer
D.E. Willmott
L. Zakuta
Lecturers
R.C. Beals
R.A. Lucas
Instructor
D.R. Pullman

1964-65
Professors
S.D. Clark (Chair)
O. Hall
R.L. James
T.H. Marshall (Visiting)
Associate Professors
J.R. Burnet
P.J. Giffen
L. Zakuta
Assistant Professors
J.J. Loubser
H.K. Nishio
D. Reuschemeyer
D.E. Willmott
Lecturers
R.C. Beals
W.D.H. Johnson

R.A. Lucas
Special Lecturer
H. Cooperstock

1965-66
Professors
S.D. Clark (Chair)
O. Hall
R.L. James
C. Tilly
Associate Professors
J.R. Burnet
P.J. Giffen
D. Reuschemeyer
D.E. Willmott
L. Zakuta
Assistant Professors
R.C. Beals
H. Cooperstock
J.J. Loubser
R.A. Lucas
H.K. Nishio
K.N. Walker
Lecturers
R.A. Carlton
I.D. Currie
W.D.H. Johnson
M.B. Scott
Special Lecturer
T.R. Maxwell

1966-67
Professors
S.D. Clark (Chair)
L.S. Feuer

25

E.K. Francis (**Visiting**)
P.J. Giffen
O. Hall
R.L. James
C. Tilly
Associate Professors
J.R. Burnet
J.J. Loubser (**Assoc. Chair**)
H.K. Nishio
D.E. Willmott
L. Zakuta
Assistant Professors
R.C. Beals
H. Cooperstock
R.A. Lucas
W. Michelson
K.N. Walker
I. Weinberg
Lecturers
R.A. Carlton
I.D. Currie
W.D.H. Johnson
Instructors
S. Cook
M. Cooper

1967-68
Professors
N.W. Bell
S.D. Clark   (**Chair**)
L.S. Feuer
E.K Francis   (**Visiting**)
P.J. Giffen
O. Hall
R.L. James
C. Tilly
Associate Professors
W.M. Gerson
J.J. Loubser (**Assoc. Chair**)
R.A. Lucas
H.K. Nishio
L. Zakuta

Assistant Professors
R.C. Baum
R.C. Beals
R. Carlton
H. Cooperstock
E.B. Harvey
J.L. Lennards
W. Michelson
K.N. Walker
I. Weinberg
B. Wellman
Lecturers
M. Cooper
I.D. Currie
M.E. Hanna
M. Kelner
A.T.R. Powell
Instructor
S. Cook

1968-69
Professors
N.W. Bell
S.D. Clark   (**Chair**)
L.S. Feuer
P.J. Giffen
O. Hall
R.L. James
J. Porter
C. Tilly
L. Zakuta
Associate Professors
R. Badgley
R. Breton
W.M. Gerson
T.D. Kemper
J.J. Loubser
R.A. Lucas
W. Michelson
H.K. Nishio
I. Weinberg   (**obiit**)

26

Assistant Professors
R.C. Baum
R.C. Beals
R. Carlton
H. Cooperstock
I.D. Currie
E.B. Harvey
J.L. Lennards
K.N. Walker
B. Wellman
Lecturers
A. Bennett
M. Cooper
M.E. Hanna
M. Kelner
A.T.R. Powell
J. Wayne
Instructors
J. Joyner
P. Weeks

1969-70
Professors
N.W. Bell
B. Blishen   (Visiting)
S.D. Clark
L.S. Feuer
P.J. Giffen   (Chair)
O. Hall
R.L. James
W. Kalbach
L. Zakuta
Associate Professors
R. Badgley
R. Breton
H. Cooperstock
W.M. Gerson
E.B. Harvey
T.D. Kemper
J.J. Loubser
R.A. Lucas
W. Michelson

H.K. Nishio
J. Wilkins
Assistant Professors
R.C. Beals
I.D. Currie
M. Kelner
J.A. Lee
J.L. Lennards
H. Makler
W. Phillips
L. Tepperman
K.N. Walker
B. Wellman
Lecturers
A. Bennett
R.W. Burnside
S. Cook
M. Cooper
M.E. Hanna
J. Joyner
R. O'Toole
A.T.R. Powell
J. Wayne
Special Lecturer
B. Baldus

1970-71
Professors
N.W. Bell
S.D. Clark
L.S. Feuer
P.J. Giffen   (Chair)
O. Hall
R.L. James
W. Kalbach
L. Zakuta
Associate Professors
R. Badgley
R. Breton
H. Cooperstock
W.M. Gerson
E.B. Harvey

W.W. Isajiw
J.J. Loubser
R.A. Lucas
W. Michelson
H.K. Nishio
K.N. Walker
J. Wilkins
Assistant Professors
B. Baldus
R.C. Beals
A. Bennett
I.D. Currie
M.E. Hanna
L. Howard
M. Kelner
J.A. Lee
J.L. Lennards
P. Lorion
D.W. Magill
H. Makler
W. Phillips
J.G. Reitz
J. Salaff
J.H. Simpson
A.H. Smith
P.H. Solomon
L. Tepperman
J. Turk
B. Wellman
Lecturers
H.J. Breslauer
R.W. Burnside
S. Cook
M. Cooper
J. Joyner
R. O'Toole
A.T.R. Powell
J. Wayne

1971-72
Professors
R. Badgley

N.W. Bell
R. Breton
S.D. Clark
L.S. Feuer
P.J. Giffen   (**Chair**)
O. Hall
R.L. James
W. Kalbach
R. Lucas
P.K. New
H. Nishio
L. Zakuta
Associate Professors
H. Cooperstock
W.M. Gerson
E.B. Harvey
W.W. Isajiw
W. Michelson
K.N. Walker
J. Wilkins
Assistant Professors
B. Baldus
R.C. Beals
A. Bennett
H.J. Breslauer
I.D. Currie
M.E. Hanna
L. Howard
M. Kelner
J.B. Kervin
J.A. Lee
J.L. Lennards
P. Lorion
D.W. Magill
H. Makler
W. Phillips
J.G. Reitz
J. Salaff
J.H. Simpson
A.H. Smith
P.H. Solomon
L. Tepperman

28

J. Turk
J. Wayne
B. Wellman
Lecturers
R.W. Burnside (**obiit**)
S. Cook
M. Cooper
J. Joyner
R. O'Toole
A.T.R. Powell
R. Rosen

1972-73
Professors
R. Badgley
N.W. Bell
R. Breton
S.D. Clark
L.S. Feuer
P.J. Giffen
O. Hall
R.L. James
W. Kalbach
R. Lucas
W. Michelson
P.K. New
H. Nishio
L. Zakuta
I.M. Zeitlin   (**Chair**)
Associate Professors
H. Cooperstock
W.M. Gerson
E.B. Harvey
W.W. Isajiw
R.W. Osborn
K.N. Walker
B. Wellman
J. Wilkins
Assistant Professors
B. Baldus
R.C. Beals
A. Bennett

H.J. Breslauer
I.D. Currie
L.F. Felt
L. Howard
L. Johnson   (**Visiting**)
M. Kelner
J.B. Kervin
J.A. Lee
J.L. Lennards
P. Lorion
D.W. Magill
H. Makler
L. Marsden   (**Visiting**)
W. Phillips
J.G. Reitz
J. Salaff
J.H. Simpson
A.H. Smith
P.H. Solomon
M.W. Spencer
L. Tepperman
J. Turk
J. Wayne
Lecturers
R.W. Burnside
S. Cook
N. Hartmann
J. Joyner
R. O'Toole
A.T.R. Powell

1973-74
Professors
R. Badgley
N.W. Bell
R. Breton
S.D. Clark
L.S. Feuer
P.J. Giffen
O. Hall
R.L. James
W. Kalbach

29

R. Lucas
W. Michelson
P.K. New
H. Nishio
K. Tsurumi   (**Visiting**)
L. Zakuta
I.M. Zeitlin   (**Chair**)
Associate Professors
H. Cooperstock
E.B. Harvey
N. Howell
W.W. Isajiw
R.W. Osborn
L. Tepperman
K.N. Walker
B. Wellman
J. Wilkins
Assistant Professors
B. Baldus
R.C. Beals
A. Bennett
H.J. Breslauer
I.D. Currie
B. Erickson
L.F. Felt
L. Howard
L. Johnson
M. Kelner
J.B. Kervin
J.A. Lee
J.L. Lennards
P. Lorion
D.W. Magill
H. Makler
L. Marsden
R. O'Toole
W. Phillips
A.T.R. Powell
J.G. Reitz
J. Salaff
J.H. Simpson
S. Small

A.H. Smith
P.H. Solomon
M.W. Spencer
J. Turk
J. Wayne
Lecturers
S. Berkowitz
N. Hartmann
J. Heap
J. Joyner
R. MacKay

1974-75
Professors
R. Badgley
N.W. Bell
R. Breton
S.D. Clark
L.S. Feuer
P.J. Giffen
O. Hall
E.B. Harvey
R.L. James
W. Kalbach
R. Lucas
W. Michelson
P.K. New
H. Nishio
H. Orbach   (**Visiting**)
P. Piccone   (**Visiting**)
J. Rex   (**Visiting**)
A.T. Turk
L. Zakuta
I.M. Zeitlin   (**Chair**)
Associate Professors
H. Boughey
H. Cooperstock
N. Howell
W.W. Isajiw
D.W. Magill
R.W. Osborn
R. Roman

30

E.Silva
L. Tepperman
K.N. Walker
B. Wellman
J. Wilkins
Assistant Professors
B. Baldus
R.C. Beals
A. Bennett
H.J. Breslauer
B. Erickson
J. Hagan
L. Howard
M. Kelner
J.B. Kervin
J.A. Lee
P. Lorion
R. MacKay
H. Makler
L. Marsden
R. O'Toole
A.T.R. Powell
J.G. Reitz
J. Salaff
J.H. Simpson
S. Small
P.H. Solomon
M.W. Spencer
J. Turk
J. Wayne
Lecturers
S. Berkowitz
M. Bodemann
J. Heap

1975-76
Professor Emeritus
O. Hall
Professors
R. Badgley
G.G. Baum
N.W. Bell

R. Breton
S.D. Clark
L.S. Feuer
P.J. Giffen
E.B. Harvey
R.L. James
W. Kalbach
R. Lucas
W. Michelson
M. Murmis   (**Visiting**)
P.K. New
H. Nishio
A.T. Turk
L. Zakuta
I.M. Zeitlin   (**Chair**)
Associate Professors
R.C. Beals
H. Boughey
D. Campbell   (**Visiting**)
H. Cooperstock
N. Howell
W.W. Isajiw
J.A. Lee
W. Leiss
D.W. Magill (**Assoc. Chair**)
R.W. Osborn
R. O'Toole
J.G. Reitz
R. Roman
J. Salaff
E. Silva
D. Smith   (**Visiting**)
L. Tepperman
K.N. Walker
B. Wellman
J. Wilkins
Assistant Professors
B. Baldus
S.D. Berkowitz
H.J. Breslauer
B. Erickson
R. Ericson

31

J. Hagan
L. Howard
M. Kelner
J.B. Kervin
P. Lorion
R. MacKay
H. Makler
L. Marsden
A.T.R. Powell
J.H. Simpson
S. Small
P.H. Solomon
M.W. Spencer
J. Turk
J. Wayne
Lecturer
M. Bodemann

1976-77
Professors Emeriti
S.D. Clark
O. Hall
Professors
R. Badgley
N.W. Bell
R. Breton
P.J. Giffen
E.B. Harvey
R.L. James
W. Kalbach
R. Lucas
W. Michelson
M. Murmis   (Visiting)
P.K. New
H. Nishio
A.T. Turk
L. Zakuta
I.M. Zeitlin   (Chair)
Associate Professors
B. Baldus
R.C. Beals
H. Boughey

D. Campbell   (**Visiting**)
H. Cooperstock
B. Erickson
N. Howell
W.W. Isajiw
J. Kervin
J.A. Lee
D.W. Magill (**Assoc. Chair**)
H. Makler
L. Marsden
R.W. Osborn
R. O'Toole
J.G. Reitz
R. Roman
J. Salaff
E. Silva
J.H. Simpson
M. Spencer
L. Tepperman
J. Turk
K.N. Walker
J. Wayne
B. Wellman
J. Wilkins
Assistant Professors
S.D. Berkowitz
H.J. Breslauer
J.L. de Lannoy
R. Ericson
B.S. Green
J. Hagan
M. Kelner
P. Lorion
R. MacKay
A.T.R. Powell
S. Small
Lecturer
M. Bodemann

1977-78
Professors Emeriti
S.D. Clark
O. Hall
Professors
R. Badgley
N.W. Bell
R. Breton
P.J. Giffen
E.B. Harvey
R.L. James
W. Kalbach
R. Lucas
W. Michelson
P.K. New
H. Nishio
A.T. Turk
L. Zakuta
I.M. Zeitlin
Associate Professors
B. Baldus
R.C. Beals
H. Boughey
D. Campbell
H. Cooperstock
J.L. de Lannoy
B. Erickson
J. Hagan
N. Howell
W.W. Isajiw
J. Kervin
J.A. Lee
D.W. Magill
H. Makler
L. Marsden   (**Chair**)
M. Murmis
R.W. Osborn
R. O'Toole
J.G. Reitz
R. Roman
J. Salaff

E. Silva
J.H. Simpson
M. Spencer
L. Tepperman
J. Turk
K.N. Walker
J. Wayne
B. Wellman
J. Wilkins
Assistant Professors
S.D. Berkowitz
M. Bodemann
R. Ericson
H. Friedmann
M. Hammond
P. Lorion
R. MacKay
A.T.R. Powell
S. Small
S. Ungar
Lecturer
D. Wagner

1978-79
Professors Emeriti
S.D. Clark
O. Hall
Professors
R. Badgley
N.W. Bell
R. Breton
P.J. Giffen
E.B. Harvey
W.W. Isajiw
R.L. James
W. Kalbach
R. Lucas   (**obiit**)
W. Michelson
P.K. New
H. Nishio
L. Tepperman
A.T. Turk

L. Zakuta
I.M. Zeitlin
Associate Professors
B. Baldus
R.C. Beals
H. Boughey
D. Campbell
H. Cooperstock
J.L. de Lannoy
B. Erickson
J. Hagan
N. Howell
J. Kervin
J.A. Lee
R. MacKay
D.W. Magill
H. Makler
L. Marsden   (**Chair**)
M. Murmis
R.W. Osborn
R. O'Toole
J.G. Reitz
R. Roman
J. Salaff
E. Silva
J.H. Simpson
M. Spencer
J. Turk
K.N. Walker
J. Wayne
B. Wellman
J. Wilkins
Assistant Professors
S.D. Berkowitz
M. Bodemann
R. Brym
R. Ericson
H. Friedmann
M. Hammond
J. Hannigan
S. Ungar

1979-80
Professors Emeriti
S.D. Clark
O. Hall
Professors
R. Badgley
G.G. Baum
N.W. Bell
R. Breton
P.J. Giffen
E.B. Harvey
N.L. Howell   (**Acting Chair**)
W.W. Isajiw
R.L. James
W. Kalbach
L. Marsden
W. Michelson
P.K. New
H. Nishio
L. Tepperman
A.T. Turk
L. Zakuta
I.M. Zeitlin
Associate Professors
B. Baldus
R.C. Beals
H. Boughey
D. Campbell
H. Cooperstock
J.L. de Lannoy
B. Erickson
R. Ericson
A.R. Gillis
J. Hagan
M. Kelner
J. Kervin
J.A. Lee
R. MacKay
D.W. Magill
H. Makler
M. Murmis
R.W. Osborn

R. O'Toole
J.G. Reitz
R. Roman
J. Salaff
E. Silva
J.H. Simpson
M. Spencer
A. Stein
J. Turk
K.N. Walker
J. Wayne
B. Wellman
J. Wilkins
Assistant Professors
S.D. Berkowitz
M. Bodemann
R. Brym
A.D. Duffy
H. Friedmann
M. Hammond
J. Hannigan
S. Ungar

1980-81
Professors Emeriti
S.D. Clark
O. Hall
Professors
R. Badgley
G.G. Baum
N.W. Bell
R. Breton
P.J. Giffen
J. Hagan
E.B. Harvey
N. Howell
W.W. Isajiw
R.L. James
W. Kalbach
L. Marsden
W. Michelson
P.K. New

H. Nishio
J.G. Reitz   (**Chair**)
L. Tepperman
A.T. Turk
B. Wellman
L. Zakuta
I.M. Zeitlin
Associate Professors
B. Baldus   (**Assoc. Chair**)
R.C. Beals
M. Bodemann
H. Boughey
R. Brym
D. Campbell
H. Cooperstock
J.L. de Lannoy
B. Erickson
R. Ericson
A.R. Gillis
M. Kelner
J. Kervin
J.A. Lee
R. MacKay
D.W. Magill
H. Makler
M. Murmis
R. O'Toole
R. Roman
J. Salaff
E. Silva
J.H. Simpson
M. Spencer
A. Stein
J. Turk
K.N. Walker
J. Wayne
J. Wilkins
Assistant Professors
S.D. Berkowitz
A.D. Duffy
H. Friedmann
M. Hammond

J. Hannigan
S. Ungar

1981-82
Professors Emeriti
S.D. Clark
O. Hall
Professors
R. Badgley
G.G. Baum
N.W. Bell
R. Breton
P.J. Giffen
J. Hagan
E.B. Harvey
N. Howell
W.W. Isajiw
R.L. James
W. Kalbach
M. Kelner
L. Marsden
W. Michelson
P.K. New
H. Nishio
J.G. Reitz   (**Chair**)
L. Tepperman
A.T. Turk
B. Wellman
L. Zakuta
I.M. Zeitlin
Associate Professors
B. Baldus   (**Assoc. Chair**)
R.C. Beals
M. Bodemann
H. Boughey
R. Brym
D. Campbell
H. Cooperstock
J.L. de Lannoy
B. Erickson
R. Ericson
H. Friedmann

A.R. Gillis
J. Kervin
J.A. Lee
R. MacKay
D.W. Magill
H. Makler
M. Murmis
R. O'Toole
R. Roman
J. Salaff
E. Silva
J.H. Simpson
M. Spencer
A. Stein
J. Turk
S. Ungar
K.N. Walker
J. Wayne
J. Wilkins
Assistant Professors
A.D. Duffy
M. Hammond
J. Hannigan
W.H. Vanderburg

1982-83
Professors Emeriti
S.D. Clark
O. Hall
Professors
R. Badgley
G.G. Baum
N.W. Bell
R. Breton
R. Ericson
P.J. Giffen
J. Hagan
E.B. Harvey
N. Howell
W.W. Isajiw
R.L. James
W. Kalbach

M. Kelner
L. Marsden
W. Michelson
P.K. New
H. Nishio
J.G. Reitz   (**Chair**)
J. Salaff
L. Tepperman
A.T. Turk
B. Wellman
L. Zakuta
I.M. Zeitlin
Associate Professors
B. Baldus   (**Assoc. Chair**)
R.C. Beals
M. Bodemann
H. Boughey
R. Brym
D. Campbell
H. Cooperstock
J.L. de Lannoy
B. Erickson
H. Friedmann
A.R. Gillis
J. Kervin
J.A. Lee
R. MacKay
D.W. Magill
H. Makler
M. Murmis
R. O'Toole
R. Roman
E. Silva
J.H. Simpson
M. Spencer
A. Stein
J. Turk
S. Ungar
K.N. Walker
J. Wayne
J. Wilkins
Assistant Professors

A.D. Duffy
M. Hammond
J. Hannigan
C. Jones
W.H. Vanderburg

1983-84
Professors Emeriti
S.D. Clark
O. Hall
Professors
R. Badgley
G.G. Baum
N.W. Bell
R. Breton
R. Ericson
P.J. Giffen
J. Hagan
E.B. Harvey
N. Howell
W.W. Isajiw
R.L. James
C. Jones
W. Kalbach
M. Kelner
L. Marsden
W. Michelson
H. Nishio
J.G. Reitz   (**Chair**)
J. Salaff
L. Tepperman
A.T. Turk
B. Wellman
L. Zakuta
I.M. Zeitlin
Associate Professors
B. Baldus   (**Assoc. Chair**)
R.C. Beals
M. Bodemann
H. Boughey
R. Brym
D. Campbell

37

H. Cooperstock
J.L. de Lannoy
B. Erickson
H. Friedmann
A.R. Gillis
M. Hammond
J. Hannigan
J. Kervin
J.A. Lee
R. MacKay
D.W. Magill
H. Makler
M. Murmis
R. O'Toole
R. Roman
E. Silva
J.H. Simpson
M. Spencer
A. Stein
J. Turk
S. Ungar
K.N. Walker
J. Wayne

Assistant Professors
A.D. Duffy
W.H. Vanderburg

1984-85
Professors Emeriti
S.D. Clark
O. Hall

Professors
R. Badgley
G.G. Baum
N.W. Bell
R. Breton
R. Ericson
P.J. Giffen
J. Hagan
E.B. Harvey
N. Howell
W.W. Isajiw

R.L. James
C. Jones
W. Kalbach
M. Kelner
L. Marsden
W. Michelson
H. Nishio
J.G. Reitz   (**Chair**)
J. Salaff
L. Tepperman
A.T. Turk
B. Wellman
L. Zakuta
I.M. Zeitlin

Associate Professors
B. Baldus   (**Assoc. Chair**)
R.C. Beals
M. Bodemann
H. Boughey
R. Brym
D. Campbell
J.L. de Lannoy
B. Erickson
H. Friedmann
A.R. Gillis
M. Hammond
J. Hannigan
J. Kervin
J.A. Lee
R. MacKay
D.W. Magill
H. Makler
M. Murmis
R. O'Toole
R. Roman
E. Silva
J.H. Simpson
M. Spencer
A. Stein
J. Turk
S. Ungar
J. Wayne

38

Assistant Professors
M. Blute
A.D. Duffy
N. Pupo
W.H. Vanderburg

1985-86
Professors Emeriti
S.D. Clark
P.J. Giffen
O. Hall
Professors
R. Badgley
G.G. Baum
N.W. Bell
R. Breton
R. Brym
B. Erickson
R. Ericson
A.R. Gillis
J. Hagan   (**Assoc. Chair**)
E.B. Harvey
N. Howell
W.W. Isajiw
R.L. James
C. Jones
W. Kalbach
M. Kelner
L. Marsden
W. Michelson
H. Nishio
R. O'Toole
J.G. Reitz
J. Salaff
L. Tepperman
A.T. Turk
B. Wellman
I.M. Zeitlin
Associate Professors
B. Baldus
R.C. Beals
M. Blute

M. Bodemann
H. Boughey
D. Campbell
J.L. de Lannoy
H. Friedmann
M. Hammond
J. Hannigan
J. Kervin
J.A. Lee
R. MacKay
D.W. Magill
H. Makler
M. Murmis
R. Roman
E. Silva
J.H. Simpson   (**Chair**)
M. Spencer
A. Stein
J. Turk
S. Ungar
J. Wayne
Assistant Professors
B. Fox
B.S. Green
C.S. Milner
N. Pupo
W.H. Vanderburg

1986-87
Professors Emeriti
S.D. Clark
P.J. Giffen
O. Hall
L. Zakuta
Professors
R. Badgley
N.W. Bell
R. Breton
R. Brym
B. Erickson
R. Ericson
A.R. Gillis

J. Hagan   (**Assoc. Chair**)
E.B. Harvey
N. Howell
W.W. Isajiw
R.L. James
C. Jones
W. Kalbach
M. Kelner
L. Marsden
W. Michelson
H. Nishio
R. O'Toole
J.G. Reitz
J. Salaff
J.H. Simpson   (**Chair**)
L. Tepperman
A.T. Turk
B. Wellman
I.M. Zeitlin
Associate Professors
B. Baldus
R.C. Beals
M. Blute
M. Bodemann
H. Boughey
D. Campbell
J.L. de Lannoy
H. Friedmann
M. Hammond
J. Hannigan
J. Kervin
J.A. Lee
R. MacKay
D.W. Magill
H. Makler
M. Murmis
R. Roman
E. Silva
M. Spencer
A. Stein
J. Turk
S. Ungar

J. Wayne
Assistant Professors
B. Fox
B.S. Green
C.S. Milner
N. Pupo
W.H. Vanderburg

1987-88
Professors Emeriti
S.D. Clark
P.J. Giffen
O. Hall
L. Zakuta
Professors
R. Badgley
N.W. Bell
R. Breton
R. Brym
B. Erickson
R. Ericson
A.R. Gillis
J. Hagan
E.B. Harvey
N. Howell
W.W. Isajiw
R.L. James
C. Jones
W. Kalbach
M. Kelner
L. Marsden
W. Michelson
H. Nishio
R. O'Toole
J.G. Reitz
J. Salaff
E. Silva
J. Simpson   (**Chair**)
L. Tepperman
A.T. Turk   (**Assoc. Chair**)
B. Wellman
I.M. Zeitlin

Associate Professors
B. Baldus
R.C. Beals
M. Blute
M. Bodemann
H. Boughey
D. Campbell
J.L. de Lannoy
H. Friedmann
M. Hammond (**Assoc. Chair**)
J. Hannigan
J. Kervin
J.A. Lee
R. MacKay
D.W. Magill
H. Makler
M. Murmis
R. Roman
M. Spencer
A. Stein
J. Turk
S. Ungar
J. Wayne
Assistant Professors
B. Fox
B.S. Green
C.S. Milner
N. Pupo
W.H. Vanderburg

Editor's Notes:

1. The basic source of information used to compile this year-by-year list of faculty members was the annual University of Toronto Faculty of Arts and Science *Calendar*. Additional information was provided by Bernd Baldus, S.D. Clark, Oswald Hall, Brenda Leblanc, John Simpson and Jeanette Wright. I would like to thank them for their help. Despite our best efforts, I have a sense of uneasiness about the accuracy of these lists. Without access to confidential personnel files, I could not verify this information, so the best claim that can be made regarding the accuracy of the yearly lists of teaching staff is that they reflect the *Calendar* listings accurately except where the *Calendar* listings were known by one of us to be incorrect and the appropriate change was made.

2. Faculty members are listed alphabetically by rank for each year. Those holding visiting appointments are designated as such in brackets following their name. The Chair and (where applicable) Associate Chair are denoted as such in bold face type in brackets after their respective name(s).

3. The list includes only those who have held regular staff appointments. Those having held sessional appointments are not listed.

CHAPTER 4

PH.D. DISSERTATIONS AND SUPERVISORS, 1963-1988

NAME	DISSERTATION TITLE (SUPERVISOR)
1966 Robin, M.	Radical Politics and Organized Labour in Canada (S.D. Clark)
1967 Carlton, R.	Differential Educational Achievement in a Bilingual Community (S.D. Clark)
1968 Crysdale, S.	Occupational and Social Mobility in Riverdale, A Blue-Collar Community (S.D. Clark)
1969 Fullan, M.	Workers' Receptivity to Industrial Change in Different Technological Settings (J. Loubser)
Kelner, M.	The Elite Structure of Toronto: Ethnic Composition and Patterns of Recruitment (S.D. Clark)
Sidlofsky, S.	Post-war Immigrants in the Changing Metropolis (J. Burnet)
1970 Turk, J.	The Measurement of Intra-Familial Power (N.W. Bell)
Weinzweig, P.	Socialization and Subculture in Elite Education: A Study of a Canadian Boys' Private School (I. Weinberg)
1971 Anderson, G.	The Channel Facilitators Model of Migration: A Model Tested Using Portuguese Blue-Collar Immigrants in Metropolitan Toronto (R. Breton)
Lodhi, A.	Urbanization, Criminality and Collective Violence: A Study in Sociology (P. Giffen)

Maidman, F.   Family Openness and Patterns of
                   Adolescent Social Engagement (N.W. Bell)
Maxwell, T.   The French Population of Metro Toronto: A
                   Study of Ethnic Participation and Ethnic
                   Identity (O. Hall)
Nkremdirim, B.   Change, Power and Conflict: A Sociological
                   Study of Collective Violence (R. Breton)
Wayne, J.   Networks of Informal Participation in a
                   Suburban Context (W. Michelson)

1972
Grayson, P.   Neighbourhood and Voting: The Social
                   Basis of Conservative Support in Broadview
                   (K. Walker)
O'Toole, R.   The Sociology of Political Sects: Four Sects
                   in Toronto in 1968-69. Vols. 1 and 2
                   (L. Feuer)
Segall, A.   Sociocultural Variation in Illness
                   Behaviour: A Comparative Study of
                   Hospitalized Anglo-Saxon Protestant and
                   Jewish Female Patients (N. Bell)
Shulman, N.   Urban Social Networks: An Investigation of
                   Personal Networks in an Urban Setting
                   (W. Michelson)
White, T.   Power and Autonomy in Organizations
                   (H.K. Nishio)

1973
Coburn, D.   Work and Society: The Social Correlates of
                   Job Control and Job Complexity (R. Badgley)
Earle, R.   The Professional Mental Patient (N.W. Bell)
Fiaz, M.   Inter-Industrial Propensity to Strike in
                   France 1890-1930 (H.K. Nishio)
Murphy, R.   The Interpenetration of Professionalism
                   and Bureaucracy (R. Breton)
Powell, A.   Participation in Issues as a Measure of
                   Integration into a Small Town (R. Breton)
Veevers, J.   Voluntary Childless Wives: An Exploratory
                   Study (N.W. Bell)

1974
Butler, P.   Involvement in Work and Family Worlds: A
                   Study of Work-Family Linkages in Single-
                   Earner and Dual-Earner Families
                   (N.W. Bell)

44

Foote, R.   A Case Study: The Social Consequences of Rapid Industrialization (R. Lucas)

Lee, D.   The Impact of Modernization and Environmental Impingements Upon Nationalism and Separatism: The Quebec Case (W.W. Isajiw)

McKie, C.   An Ontario Industrial Elite: The Senior Executive In Manufacturing Industry (L. Felt)

Pepperdene, B.   The Occupation of Nursing and Careers: A Study of the Careers of Diploma and Degree Nurses (O. Hall)

Strilaeff, F.   Turnover of Nurses in Hospitals: A Study of a Service Organization (R. Badgley)

1975

Clavir, J.   "Better Conquer Hearts than Citadels": A Study in the Sociology of Culture and Social Change in Viet Nam (I.M. Zeitlin)

Erinosho, A.   Socio-Psychiatric Attributes and Therapeutic Structures as Predictors of Post-Hospital Performance: A Study of Two Psychiatric Centres in Nigeria (N.W. Bell)

Himmelfarb, A.   Fat Man, Thin World: A Participant Observation Study of Weight Watchers (L. Zakuta)

Kennedy, L.   Residential Mobility as a Cyclical Process: The Evaluation of the Home Environment both Before and After the Move (W. Michelson)

Klein, W.   Judicial Recruitment in Manitoba, Ontario and Quebec, 1905-1970 (P.J. Giffen)

1976

Brym, R.   Strangers and Rebels: The Russian-Jewish Intelligensia in Marxist Social Movements at the Turn of the Twentieth Century (I.M. Zeitlin)

D'Arcy, K.   Change and Consequence in a Mental Health System: Theoretical and Empirical Chapters in a Sociology of Mental Illness (R. Badgley)

Djao, A.	Social Control in a Colonial Society: A Case Study of Working Class Consciousness in Hong Kong (B.Baldus)
Ehrentraut, A.	Technology and the Japanese Worker (H.K. Nishio)
Fetterley, R.	Owners and Trainers: Patterns of Establishing and Maintaining Autonomy in a Worker-Client Relationship (O. Hall)
Gerber, L.	Minority Survival: Community Characteristics and Out-Migration from Indian Communities Across Canada (R. Breton)
Glickman, Y.	Organizational Indicators and Social Correlates of Collective Jewish Identity. Vols. 1 and 2 (R. Breton)
Konzak, B.	Retirement and Aging in Canadian Society (H.K. Nishio)
Makabe, T.	Ethnic Group Identity: Canadian-Born Japanese in Metropolitan Toronto (W.W. Isajiw)
Newson, J.	The Roman-Catholic Clerical Exodus: A Study of Role Adaptation and Organizational Change (R. Breton)
Plange, A.	The Colonial State and Underdevelopment (J. Wayne)
Reed, P.	Life Style as an Element of Social Logic: Patterns of Activity, Social Characteristics, and Residential Choice (W. Michelson)
Sacouman, J.	Social Origins of Antigonish Movement Co-operative Associations in Eastern Nova Scotia (D. Magill)
Trenton, T.	Canadian Identity and Nationalism Among University Students: An Exploratory Analysis of the Applicability of Current Theory on Student Protest (K. Walker)

1977

Adam, B.	Social Psychology of Inferiorized People (B. Baldus)
Blute, M.	Darwinian Analogues and the Naturalistic Explanation of Purpose in Biology, Psychology, and the Sociocultural Sciences (W.W. Isajiw)

Boudreau-Lemieux, F.	Changes in the System for the Distribution of Psychiatric Care in Quebec, 1960-1974 (N.W. Bell)
Carveth, D.	Sociologism and Psychoanalysis: A Study of Implicit Theories of Human Nature in "Symbolic Interactionism", "Reality Constructionism" and Psychoanalysis (L. Zakuta)
Christy, R.	Social Change and Post-Modernity: An Analysis of Social Space and Social Time in Canada and the United States (W. Michelson)
Cohen, R.	The Impact of Work-Setting on Clinical Training of Medical Students (P.K. New)
Connidis, I.	A Theoretical Development of Social Systems Analysis and an Examination of its Applicability to the Criminal Justice System (P.J. Giffen)
Derow, E.	Married Women's Employment and Domestic Labour (W. Michelson)
Hammond, M.	The Rise of the Pre-sapiens Theory in British and French Paleontology: A Study in the Sociology of Scientific Ideas (W.W. Isajiw)
Lundy, K.	The Effect of Organizational Setting on Secretary-Executive Interaction (P.K. New)
Martens, H.	The Relationship of Religious to Socio-Economic Divisions Among the Mennonites of Dutch-Prussian-Russian Descent in Canada (S.D. Clark)
Petrunik, M.	The Quest for Fluency: A Study of the Identity Problems and Manangement Strategies of Adult Stutterers and Some Suggestions for an Approach to the Management of Deviance (L. Zakuta)
Schwartz, R.	Utopia and Critical Theory (I.M. Zeitlin)
Shearing, C.	Real Men, Wise Men, Good Men and Cautious Men: A Study of Culture, Role Models and Interaction within a Police Communications Centre (L. Zakuta)

Snider, L.   Does the Legal System Reflect the Power Structure: A Test of Conflict Theory (A. Turk)

Subramaniam, I. Identity-Shift: Post-Migration Changes in Identity Among First-Generation East Indian Immigrants in Toronto (W.W. Isajiw)

Wilson, S.   The Changing Image of Canadian Women as Reflected in Popular Magazines, 1931-1970 (L. Tepperman)

1978

Brannigan, A.   A Study of the Social Organization of Discoveries in Science (J. Turk)

Cape, E.   "Going Downhill": Responses to Terminality in a Population of Institutionalized Aged Ill (R.L. James)

Craven, P.   "An Impartial Umpire": Industrial Relations and the Canadian State, 1900-1911 (B.Baldus)

Effrat, M.   Social Order and Unsocialized Behaviour: A Sociological Study of Privacy (W.W. Isajiw)

Gilmore, A.   Crowding: An Anatomy of a Spurious Paradigm (W. Michelson)

Harris, M.   Social Order and Individualized Behaviour: A Sociological Study of Privacy (W.W. Isajiw)

Parakulam, G.   Physical Density, Perceived Crowding and Reproductive Orientation (W. Kalbach)

Runge, J.   Progressive Educational Reform in Comparative Perspective (L.R. Marsden)

Russell, S.   Sex Role Socialization in the High School: A Study of the Perpetuation of Patriarchal Culture (R. Breton)

Torrance, G.   The Underside of the Hospital: Recruitment and the Meaning of Work Among Non-Professional Hospital Workers (P.K. New)

1979

Bakker, H.   Patrimonialism and Imperialism as Factors in Underdevelopment: A Comparative Historical Sociological Analysis of Java with Emphasis on Aspects

	of the Cultivation System, 1830-1870 (I.M. Zeitlin)
Currie, A.	Intra-Ethnic Marriage and Identification among German and Ukrainian Ethnic Groups in Canada: A Study of the Effect of Socioeconomic Status on Structural Ethnic Identification (W. Kalbach)
Deutschmann, L.	Decline of the WASP?: Dominant Group Identity in a Multi-ethnic Society (W.W. Isajiw)
Gibbons, J.	Artists, Dealers and Hustlers: The Art of Business or the Business of Art (R. Badgley)
Giffin, K.	Opportunities and Ideologies: Women in High-Status Professions in Bahia, Brazil (B. Baldus)
Huxley, C.	The Institutionalization of Industrial Conflict: A Comparative Analysis of Strike Activity in Britain and Canada since 1945 (D. Magill)
Lowe, G.	The Administrative Revolution: The Growth of Clerical Occupations and the Development of the Modern Office in Canada, 1911-1931 (D. Magill)
Murray, S.	Social Science Networks (D. Magill)
Rhyne, D.	Organizational Life in River City: A Case Study of Class, Ethnicity, Geographical Mobility and Status (J. Turk)
Trottier, C.	Teachers as Agents of Political Socialization (R. Breton)

1980

Curtis, B.	The Political Economy of Elementary Educational Development: Comparative Perspectives on State Schooling in Upper Canada (J. Wayne)
Donaldson, B.	Cultural Legitimacy in the Australian Art World: A Study in the Sociology of Cultural Production (L. Zakuta)
Farrelly, R.	The Large Landowners of England and Wales, 1870-1939: An Elite in Transition (R. O'Toole)
Giesbrecht, N.	Changes in the Drinking Patterns of Skid Row Alcoholics: A Study in the Sociology of

	the Normalization of Deviants. Vols. 1 and 2 (P.J. Giffen)
MacLeod, H.	The Transformation of the United Church of Canada, 1946-1977: A Study in the Sociology of the Denomination (R. O'Toole)
McKendy, J.	Max Weber and the Sociology of Roman Catholicism (I.M. Zeitlin)
Milner, C.	God, Saints, and Spirits: A Comparative Analysis of Brazilian Urban Medical Systems (P.K. New)
Riggins, S.	Institutional Change in Nineteenth-Century French Music (D. Magill)
Sarginson, G.	Explanation, Description and Historical Phenomena: A Critique of Organismic and Atomistic Theoretical Models in the Social Sciences (B. Erickson)
Siddique, J.	Work and Family in Contemporary Industrial Society: An Analysis of Canadian Data (J. Turk)
Smith, R.D.	Social Class and Health Behaviour. Vols. 1 and 2 (R. Badgley)
Van Vliet, W.	Use, Evaluation and Knowledge of City and Suburban Environments by Children of Employed and Non-Employed Mothers (W. Michelson)

1981

Allahar, A.	Ideology and Practice: The Responses of the Cuban Sugar Planters to the Political and Economic Challenges of the 19th Century (M. Murmis)
Carrington, P.	Horizontal Co-optation Through Comparative Interlocks (L. Tepperman)
Edgington, B.	The Formation of the Asylum in Upper Canada (N.W. Bell)
Laxer, G.	The Social Origins of Canada's Branch-Plant Economy 1837-1914. Vols. 1 and 2 (D. Magill)
Listiak, A.	Corporate Power and the Market: Automotive Performance and the Automobile Industry. Vols. 1 and 2 (A. Turk)

Meier, P.	The Peasant Craftsmen of Otavalo, Ecuador (M. Murmis)
Pilotta, J.	Lived Nature and Self-Production: A Phenomenology of the Sensuous Universal (R. Mackay)
Storey, R.	Workers, Unions and Steel: The Shaping of the Hamilton Working Class, 1935-1948 (J. Turk)
Winson, A.	Estate Agriculture, Capitalist Development and the State: The Specificity of Contemporary Costa Rica (M. Murmis)

1982

Anderson, K.	Huron Women and Huron Men: The Effects of Demography, Kinship and the Social Division of Labour on Male/Female Relations Among the 17th-Century Huron (J. Wayne)
Baker, R.	Collaboration and Conflict: Scientific Change and the Structure of Biomedical Research (L. Marsden)
Cheung, Y.	The Social Organization of Missionary Medicine: A Study of Two Canadian Protestant Missions in China Before 1937 (P.K. New)
Corman, J.	The Impact of State Ownership on a State Proprietary Corporation: The Potash Corporation of Saskatchewan (B. Wellman)
Dasko, D.	Incomes, Income Attainment and Income Inequality Among Race-Sex Groups: A Test of the Dual Industry Theory (J. Reitz)
Dickinson, J.	Regulating the Uncertainties of Industrial Life: A Comparative Analysis of the Origins of Social Insurance in Britain and Germany, 1870-1914. Vols. 1 and 2 (J. Wayne)
Knutilla, M.	The Impact of the Western Canadian Agrarian Movement on Federal Government Policy, 1900-1930: An Assessment and Analysis (R. Brym)
Mann, S.	Obstacles to Capitalist Development of Agriculture: An Analysis of the Class

	Structure and Uneven Development of Capitalist Agriculture, 1870-1930 (J. Wayne)
McAllister, H.	Labour and the State: The Canadian Labour Congress, Consultative Forums, and Incomes Policies, 1960-1978 (J. Turk)
McDermott, P.	Computers and Multinational Corporate Management Strategies (B. Baldus)
Morgan, C.	Therapeutic Solutions to Deviance: The Social Organization of Treating Disturbed Young People (R. Mackay)
Mostacci-Calzavara, L.	Social Networks and Access to Job Opportunity (J. Reitz)
Stasiulis, D.	Race, Ethnicity and the State: The Political Structuring of South Asian and West Indian Communal Action in Combatting Racism (R. Breton)

1983

Ghorayshi, P.	Agricultural Development in Quebec: An Analysis of Production Units in the Agrarian Class Structure (I.M. Zeitlin)
Minai, K.	Continuity and Modernization in Postwar Japan: A Comparative Analysis of Farmers and Urban Employees (H.K. Nishio)
O'Hearn, M.	The Political Transformation of a Religious Order (D. Magill)
Schenk, C.	Massey Workers and Wage Controls: A Case Study of Mobilization and Coercive Integration (R. Roman)
Tippin, D.	The Legitimation of Social Change: Ontario Railways and the Idea of Progress, 1841-1884 (B. Baldus)

1984

Dajani, S.	Health Care and Development: A Case Study of the Israeli-Occupied West Bank. Vols. 1 and 2 (R. Badgley)
Gannagé, C.	Dividing Women and Men: The Role of the Company, the Union and the Family in a Canadian Garment Factory (J. Turk)
Jensen, P.	Collective Bargaining of Nurses in Canada. Vols. 1, 2 and 3 (R. Badgley)

Richardson, J. A "Structural Rational" Theory of Financial-Nonfinancial Directorship Interlocks (L. Tepperman)

Walters, R. Colonial Administrative Structures and Socio-Economic Development in the Island of Trinidad, 1498-1783 (I.M. Zeitlin)

1985

Boritch, Helen The Making of Toronto the Good: The Organization of Policing and Production of Arrests, 1859-1955 (J. Hagan)

Gross, P. Kinship Structures in Remarriage Families (M. Eichler)

Helmes-Hayes, R. Images of Inequality in Early Canadian Sociology, 1922-1965. Vols. 1 and 2 (B. Baldus)

Ityavyar, D. The Development of Health Services in Nigeria, 1960-1985 (J. Wayne)

Menzies, R. Doing Violence: Psychiatric Discretion and the Prediction of Dangerousness. Vols. 1 and 2 (R. Erickson)

Reiter, E. Out of the Frying Pan and Into the Fryer: The Organization of Work in a Fast Food Outlet (J. Turk)

1986

Beamish, R. A Study of Marx's Intellectual Labour Process: The Case of the Division of Labour (M. Murmis)

Benjamin, M. The Organization of the Child Protective Service System in Metropolitan Toronto, 1978-81: The Negotiation of Disorder (N.W. Bell)

Chunn, D. From Punishment to Doing Good: The Origins and Impact of Family Courts in Ontario, 1888-1942 (R. Ericson)

Hiscott, R. Transcending the Marginal Work World: A Sociological Analysis of Migration between Atlantic Canada and Ontario (D. Magill)

Leighton, B. Examining Personal Network Communities (B. Wellman)

Murphy, C. The Social and Formal Organization of Small Town Policing: A Comparative

	Analysis of R.C.M.P. and Municipal Policing (R. Ericson)
Nauratil, Jr., K.	Labor, Patronage and Social Structure in the Making of Medieval Architecture: France and England, 1000-1300 (I.M. Zeitlin)
O'Connor, J.	Public Welfare Expenditure and Policy Orientation in O.E.C.D. Countries, 1960-1980 (R. Brym)
Owomero, B.	Crime Trends and Patterns of Three African Countries, 1960-1979 (A. Turk)
Vaitkus, S.	Intersubjectivity and the Social Group: An Investigation into Intersubjectivity as a Problem of the Social Group Based Upon the Works of George Herbert Mead, Aron Gurwitsch and Alfred Schutz (R. Mackay)
Visano, L.	Staging a Deviant Career: The Social Organization of Male Street Prostitution (D. Magill)
Wilson, M.	Mexico's Oil Workers: Incorporation and Insurgency (R. Roman)

1987

Asbury, K.	Embedded Social Control: A Study of the Role of the Apartment Superintendent (P.J. Giffen)
Bryant, J.	Moral Codes and Social Structure in Ancient Greece: A Study on the Social Origins of Greek Ethics from Homer to the Epicureans and Stoics. Vols. 1 and 2 (I.M. Zeitlin)
Hanson, B.	Attempts to Model Context: Senile Dementia in the Family as a Case Demonstration (N.W. Bell)
Malarkey, R.	The Emergence of Equal Pay Legislation in Ontario (J. Hagan)
Martin, M.	Communication and Social Forms: A Study of the Development of the Telephone System, 1876-1920 (J. Wayne)

1988

Benoit, C.	Midwives in Passage: A Case Study of Occupational Change (R. Brym)

Jackson, L.   In Whose Interests? A Study of Canadian
                    Bilateral Aid to Jamaica's Agricultural
                    Sector (M. Murmis)

Editor's Note:
Where possible, the list of Ph.D.s awarded 1963-1988 was
compiled by direct reference to the dissertations on file in the
University of Toronto Department of Sociology Library.
Information not available there was compiled from
Departmental files by Jeanette Wright. I want to thank her for
her help.

The dates noted are those found on the cover of the dissertation
in question.

Note the following breakdown of dissertations by year (figure in
bracket is a cumulative total):

Year	Count	(Cumulative)
1963	0	
1964	0	
1965	0	
1966	1	
1967	1	(2)
1968	1	(3)
1969	3	(6)
1970	2	(8)
1971	6	(14)
1972	5	(19)
1973	6	(25)
1974	6	(31)
1975	5	(36)
1976	14	(50)
1977	17	(67)
1978	10	(77)
1979	10	(87)
1980	12	(99)
1981	9	(108)
1982	13	(121)
1983	5	(126)
1984	5	(131)
1985	6	(137)
1986	12	(149)
1987	5	(154)
1988	2	(156) (partial total)

Prior to 1963, nine Ph.D.s had been awarded in sociology, the first in 1925 (for a complete list, see Appendix B). In the first three years after the establishment of the Department in 1963, there were no Ph.D.s granted. Indeed, only eight were awarded in the first eight years of its existence. A pattern then developed such that five or six Ph.D.s were awarded during each of the next five years (1971-1975). Then, all of a sudden, in 1976 and 1977, the Department awarded 14 and 17 Ph.D.s, respectively; almost doubling the Department's previous output in two years (from 36 to 67). Indeed, in the five year period between 1976 and 1980 the Department awarded 63 or 64 percent of the 100 Ph.D.s it had given out to that point and 40 percent of the 156 it has given out in its twenty-five year history. Since 1980 the Department has, with two exceptions (1982, 1986), returned to its usual yearly rate of production.

LIST OF TEACHING STAFF
BY YEAR PRIOR TO 1963-64*

1934-35

E.J. Urwick	Professor of Economics
J.D. Ketchum	Assistant Professor of Psychology
C.W.M. Hart	Lecturer in Anthropology

1935-36

E.J. Urwick	Professor of Economics
J.D. Ketchum	Assistant Professor of Psychology
C.W.M. Hart	Lecturer in Anthropology and Supervisor of Studies in Sociology

1936-37

E.J. Urwick	Professor of Economics
J.D. Ketchum	Assistant Professor of Psychology
C.W.M. Hart	Assistant Professor of Anthropology and Supervisor of Studies in Sociology
S.D. Clark	Instructor

1937-38

E.J. Urwick	Professor Emeritus
J.D. Ketchum	Assistant Professor of Psychology
C.W.M. Hart	Assistant Professor of Anthropology and Supervisor of Studies in Sociology
J.G. Franz	Instructor in Sociology

1938-39

E.J. Urwick	Professor Emeritus
J.D. Ketchum	Assistant Professor of Psychology
C.W.M. Hart	Assistant Professor of Anthropology and Supervisor of Studies in Sociology
S.D. Clark	Lecturer in Sociology

1939-40
E.J. Urwick   Professor Emeritus
C.W.M. Hart   Assistant Professor of Sociology
J.D. Ketchum   Assistant Professor of Psychology
S.D. Clark   Lecturer in Sociology

1940-41
E.J. Urwick   Professor Emeritus
C.W.M. Hart   Assistant Professor of Sociology
J.D. Ketchum   Assistant Professor of Psychology
S.D. Clark   Lecturer in Sociology
E.C. Devereux   Instructor in Sociology

1941-42*
C.W.M. Hart   Assistant Professor
S.D. Clark   Lecturer
E.C. Devereux   Instructor
[Editor's Note: Beginning in 1941-42 all appointments are in sociology]

1942-43
C.W.M. Hart   Assistant Professor
S.D. Clark   Lecturer
A.D. Ross   Instructor

1943-44
C.W.M. Hart   Assistant Professor
S.D. Clark   Lecturer
A.D. Ross   Instructor
E.R. Younge   Instructor

1944-45
C.W.M. Hart   Associate Professor
S.D. Clark   Assistant Professor
D.G. Marshall   Lecturer
A.D. Ross   Instructor

1945-46
C.W.M. Hart   Associate Professor
S.D. Clark   Assistant Professor
J.R. Burnet   Instructor
P.J. Giffen   Instructor

1946-47

C.W.M. Hart	Associate Professor
S.D. Clark	Assistant Professor
S.M. Lipset	Lecturer
J.R. Burnet	Instructor

1947-48

C.W.M. Hart	Associate Professor
S.D. Clark	Assistant Professor
J.R. Burnet	Lecturer
E. Chinoy	Lecturer
S.M. Lipset	Lecturer
S.T. Wargon	Teaching Fellow

1948-49

S.D. Clark	Associate Professor
E. Chinoy	Lecturer
P.J. Giffen	Lecturer
J.W. Watson	Instructor
S.T. Wargon	Teaching Fellow

1949-50

S.D. Clark	Associate Professor
J.R. Burnet	Lecturer
E. Chinoy	Lecturer
P.J. Giffen	Lecturer
D.R. Pullman	Teaching Fellow

1950-51

S.D. Clark	Associate Professor
J.R. Seeley	Associate Professor (part-time)
R.A. Sim	Assistant Professor (part-time)
J.R. Burnet	Lecturer
E. Chinoy	Lecturer
P.J. Giffen	Lecturer
D.R. Pullman	Instructor

1951-52

T.J. Geiger	Professor (Visiting)
S.D. Clark	Associate Professor
J.R. Seeley	Associate Professor (part-time)
R.A. Sim	Assistant Professor (part-time)

J.R. Burnet   Lecturer
P.J. Giffen   Lecturer
J.C. Riemersma   Lecturer
N.B. Ryder   Lecturer

1952-53
S.D. Clark   Associate Professor
J.R. Seeley   Associate Professor (part-time)
R.A. Sim   Assistant Professor (part-time)
J.R. Burnet   Lecturer
J.C. Riemersma   Lecturer
N.B. Ryder   Lecturer
L. Zakuta   Lecturer

1953-54
S.D. Clark   Professor
J.R. Seeley   Associate Professor (part-time)
R.A. Sim   Assistant Professor (part-time)
J.R. Burnet   Lecturer
P.J. Giffen   Lecturer
N.B. Ryder   Lecturer
L. Zakuta   Lecturer

1954-55
S.D. Clark   Professor
J.R. Burnet   Assistant Professor
P.J. Giffen   Lecturer
L. Zakuta   Lecturer
R.E.L. Watson   Instructor

1955-56
S.D. Clark   Professor
J.R. Burnet   Assistant Professor
P.J. Giffen   Assistant Professor
D.H. Wrong   Lecturer
L. Zakuta   Lecturer
W.E. Mann   Instructor

1956-57
S.D. Clark   Professor
O. Hall   Professor
J.R. Burnet   Assistant Professor

P.J. Giffen   Assistant Professor
M.N. Richter   Lecturer
L. Zakuta   Lecturer

1957-58
S.D. Clark   Professor
O. Hall   Professor
J.R. Burnet   Assistant Professor
P.J. Giffen   Assistant Professor
L. Zakuta   Lecturer

1958-59
S.D. Clark   Professor
O. Hall   Professor
J.R. Burnet   Assistant Professor
P.J. Giffen   Assistant Professor
L. Zakuta   Lecturer

1959-60
S.D. Clark   Professor
O. Hall   Professor
N. Keyfitz   Professor
J.R. Burnet   Assistant Professor
P.J. Giffen   Assistant Professor
L. Zakuta   Assistant Professor

1960-61
S.D. Clark   Professor
O. Hall   Professor
N. Keyfitz   Professor
Sir A. Carr-Saunders   Professor (Visiting)
J.R. Burnet   Assistant Professor
P.J. Giffen   Assistant Professor
L. Zakuta   Assistant Professor
B.A. McFarlane   Special Lecturer
D.G. Hill   Instructor

1961-62
S.D. Clark   Professor
O. Hall   Professor
N. Keyfitz   Professor
J.R. Burnet   Assistant Professor

P.J. Giffen	Assistant Professor
L. Zakuta	Assistant Professor
H.K. Nishio	Special Lecturer

1962-63

S.D. Clark	Professor
O. Hall	Professor
N. Keyfitz	Professor
P.J. Giffen	Associate Professor
J.R. Burnet	Assistant Professor
L. Zakuta	Assistant Professor
R.C. Beals	Lecturer
R.J. Coughlin	Special Lecturer
R.A. Lucas	Special Lecturer
D.E. Willmott	Instructor

* *Editor's Note*: This appendix is based on "The Staff in Sociology", an unpublished manuscript (n.d.) compiled by S.D. Clark. I double-checked Professor Clark's list by doing an independent review of the *Calendar* listings and then discussing discrepancies with Professor Clark. I would like to thank him for his help.

PH.D. DISSERTATIONS IN SOCIOLOGY COMPLETED PRIOR TO 1963*

1925	Fisher, Helen E.	Professional Associations in Canada.
1926	Cheng, Tien-Fang	Oriental Immigration in Canada.
1929	Cotton, Lorna E.	The Principle of Group Activity.
1932	Hamilton, Catherine R.	Education in the Life of the People: A Study of its Place in the Social Life of Modern England
1937	Bryce, Lucy W.	The Changing Family in India
1953	Mann, William E.	Sect and Cult in Alberta
1960	Hill, Daniel G.	Negroes in Toronto: A Sociological Study of a Minority Group
1960	Pullman, Douglas R.	A Study of Social Organization in Relation to Economic Change
1960	Watson, R.E.L.	The Nova Scotia Teachers' Union: A Study in the Sociology of Formal Organizations

* *Editor's Note*: This material was *taken from a bibliography by Judy Mills and Irene Dombra, University of Toronto Doctoral Theses, 1897-1967* (Toronto: University of Toronto Press, 1968: 137-8).